LV

D1442563

SIMPLE MACHINES

Levers

by Kay Manolis

BELLWETHER MEDIA • MINNEAPOLIS, MN

Note to Librarians, Teachers, and Parents:

Blastoff! Readers are carefully developed by literacy experts and combine standards-based content with developmentally appropriate text.

Level 1 provides the most support through repetition of high-frequency words, light text, predictable sentence patterns, and strong visual support.

Level 2 offers early readers a bit more challenge through varied simple sentences, increased text load, and less repetition of high-frequency words.

Level 3 advances early-fluent readers toward fluency through increased text and concept load, less reliance on visuals, longer sentences, and more literary language.

Level 4 builds reading stamina by providing more text per page, increased use of punctuation, greater variation in sentence patterns, and increasingly challenging vocabulary.

Level 5 encourages children to move from "learning to read" to "reading to learn" by providing even more text, varied writing styles, and less familiar topics.

Whichever book is right for your reader, Blastoff! Readers are the perfect books to build confidence and encourage a love of reading that will last a lifetime!

This edition first published in 2010 by Bellwether Media, Inc.

No part of this publication may be reproduced in whole or in part without written permission of the publisher. For information regarding permission, write to Bellwether Media, Inc., Attention: Permissions Department, Post Office Box 19349, Minneapolis, MN 55419.

Library of Congress Cataloging-in-Publication Data
Manolis, Kay.
  Levers / by Kay Manolis.
    p. cm. — (Blastoff! readers. Simple machines)
  Includes bibliographical references and index.
  Summary: "Simple text, full color photographs, and illustrations introduce beginning readers to the basic principles of levers. Developed by literary experts for students in grades 2 through 5"—Provided by publisher.
  ISBN 978-1-60014-325-0 (hardcover : alk. paper)
  1. Levers—Juvenile literature. I. Title.

TJ147.M227 2010
621.8—dc22   2009008269

Contents

What Is a Lever?

Have you ever used a rake to gather leaves? A rake is a **lever**. It helps you move leaves into piles. A lever is a **simple machine**. A simple machine has few or no moving parts. Simple machines help people move objects called **loads** from one place to another. This is called doing **work**.

How Levers Work

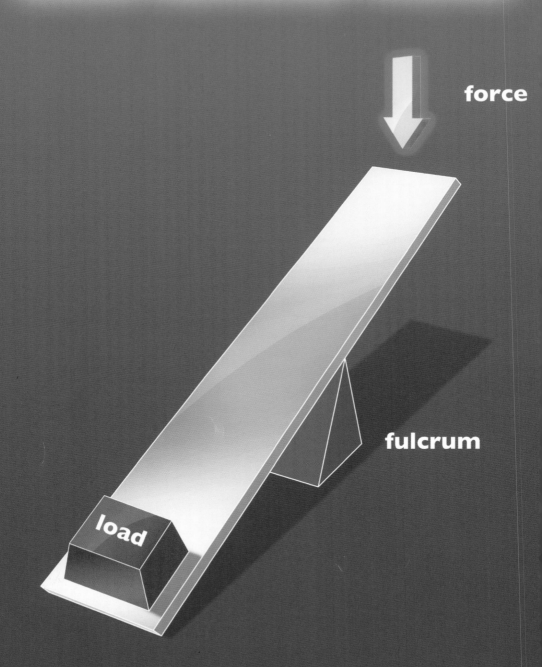

force

fulcrum

load

A lever is a bar that turns on a point called the **fulcrum**. The fulcrum does not move. When you push down or lift one part of a lever, another part of the lever moves a load. All types of work, like pushing, pulling, or lifting, require **force**. The amount of force needed to do work is called **effort**.

Levers have many uses. They help lift heavy loads. They pry open boxes and containers. They move objects faster and farther.

Some levers are just a straight bar, such as a shovel. Other levers are more complicated. A pair of scissors is two levers joined together at the fulcrum.

fun fact

The word *lever* comes from a French word that means "to raise."

Classes of Levers

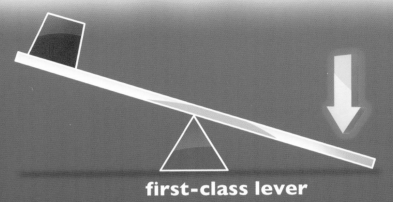

first-class lever

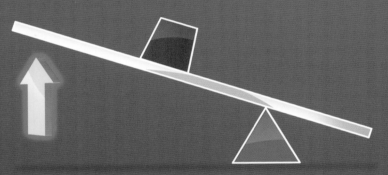

second-class lever

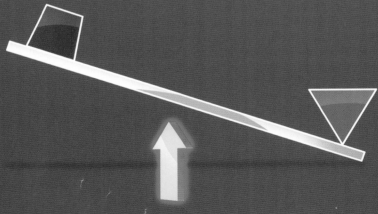

third-class lever

There are three classes of levers. They are called **first-class levers**, **second-class levers**, and **third-class levers**. The differences between these types are the locations of the fulcrums and the loads, and where you apply force. These levers do different kinds of jobs, but they all make work easier.

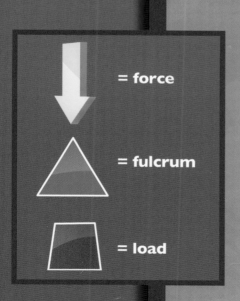

= force

= fulcrum

= load

A seesaw is a first-class lever. The fulcrum is in the middle of a seesaw. When you are on the ground, you are the load. When you are at the top, **gravity** is the force pulling you down. The force and the load move in opposite directions. Both people on a seesaw take turns lifting each other off the ground.

fun fact

Some animals use first-class levers. Orangutans use sticks to pry open fruit.

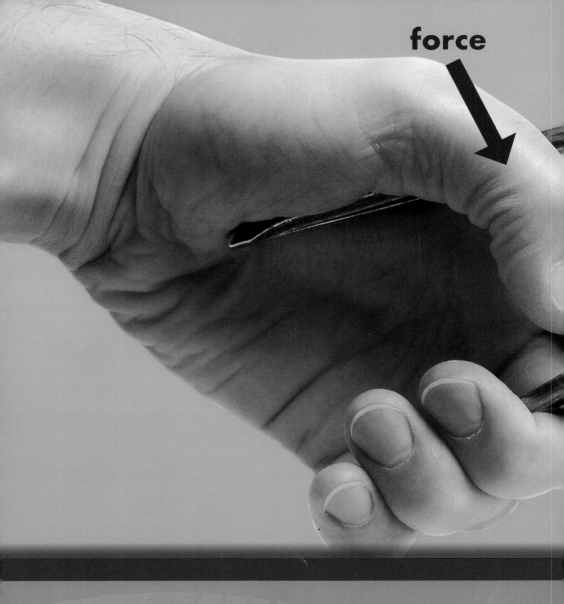

force

A nutcracker is a second-class lever.
The fulcrum is at one end of the nutcracker.
You squeeze the handles on the other end
to apply force. The nut is the load. It is
placed between the fulcrum and the force.

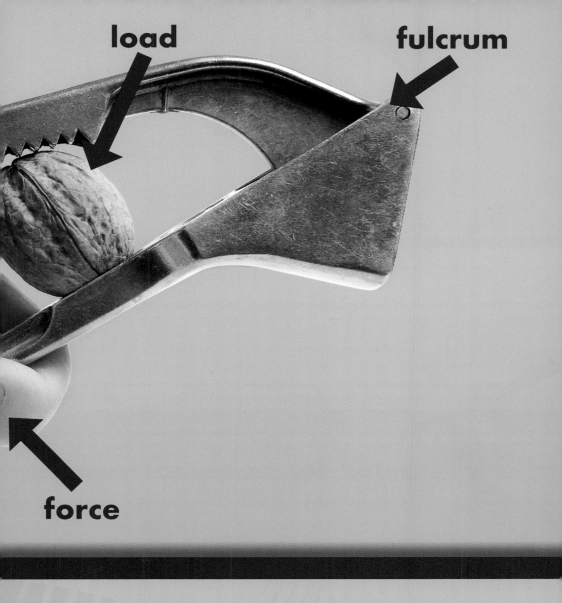

load

fulcrum

force

In second-class levers, the load moves in the same direction as the force. As a nut is squeezed in a nutcracker, its shell cracks inward.

You can make work easier with first-class and second-class levers by moving a large load closer to the fulcrum. When two people with different weights want to ride a seesaw, the heavier person should move closer to the center. This makes it easier for the light rider to lift the heavy one.

force

fulcrum

load

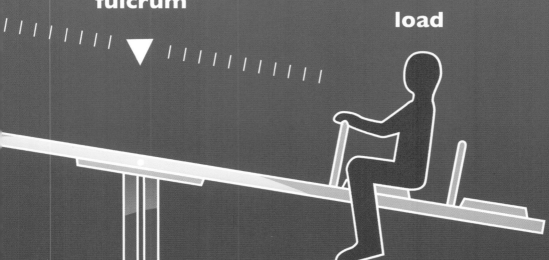

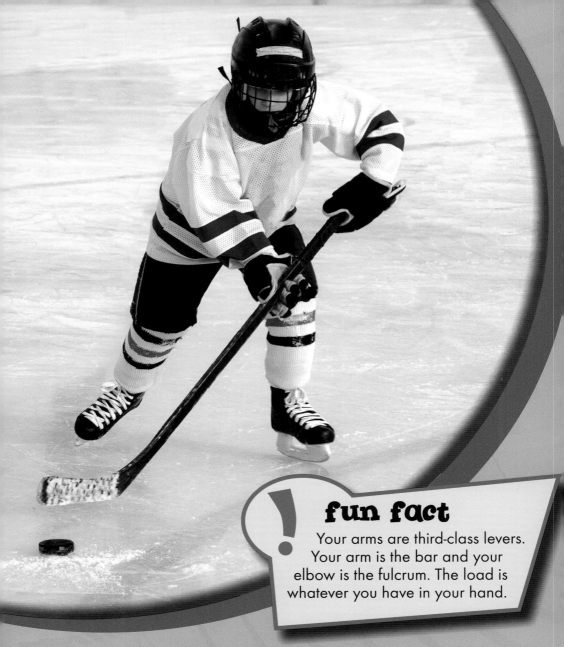

Third-class levers are used in many sports. Baseball bats and hockey sticks are third-class levers. The force is applied between the load and the fulcrum.

The batter's hands are the fulcrum, the baseball is the load, and force is applied between the hands and the baseball. The load always moves in the same direction as the force. A ball moves fast and far when you hit it with a lever!

Levers and Complex Machines

Levers are often parts of **complex machines**. A complex machine is made of two or more simple machines that work together. A skateboard is a complex machine. The board is the lever. The fulcrums are located where the wheels attach to the board. A rider pushes down on one of the fulcrums to do tricks!

! fun fact

A kick turn is a common move used by skateboarders. Riders balance on the rear wheels and spin around.

Glossary

complex machine—a machine made of two or more simple machines that work together

effort—the amount of force needed to move an object from one place to another

first-class lever—a type of lever where the fulcrum is between the load and the force

force—a push or pull that causes an object to move, change its direction, or stop moving

fulcrum—the fixed point of a lever

gravity—the force that pulls objects down toward the surface of the earth

lever—a simple machine made up of a bar that moves around a fixed point called a fulcrum

load—an object moved by a machine

second-class lever—a type of lever where the load is between the fulcrum and the force

simple machine—a machine that has few or no moving parts

third-class lever—a type of lever where the force is between the fulcrum and the load

work—to move a load from one place to another

To Learn More

AT THE LIBRARY
Gardner, Robert. *Sensational Science Projects with Simple Machines.* Berkley Heights, N.J.: Enslow, 2006.

Hewitt, Sally. *Machines We Use.* New York, N.Y.: Children's Press, 1998.

Welsbacher, Anne. *Levers.* Mankato, Minn.: Coughlan, 2000.

ON THE WEB
Learning more about simple machines is as easy as 1, 2, 3.

1. Go to www.factsurfer.com.

2. Enter "simple machines" into the search box.

3. Click the "Surf" button and you will see a list of related Web sites.

With factsurfer.com, finding more information is just a click away.

Index

The images in this book are reproduced through the courtesy of: Thomas J. Peterson / Getty Images, front cover; Image Source / Getty Images, pp. 4-5; Jon Eppard, pp. 6-7, 10-11, 16-17; Tony Anderson / Getty Images, p. 8; Nina Shannon, p. 9; Gary Rhijnsburger / Masterfile, pp. 12-13; Glo, pp. 14-15; Lorraine Swanson, p. 18; Ronald Manera, p. 19; Guillermo Trejos, pp. 20-21.